# Steelhead Fly Fishing

## In Low Water

### *a different approach*

**new fly designs, techniques & reflections**

# Steelhead Fly Fishing
## In Low Water
*a different approach*

new fly designs, techniques & reflections
*By Dick Van Demark*
**with the photography of Ralph Wahl**

Forrest Park Publishers
Bellingham, Washington

Forrest Park Publishers
P.O. Box 29775
Bellingham, Washington
98228-1775
(360) 647-2505


PRINTED IN THE UNITED STATES OF AMERICA


**ISBN:** 1-879522-05-5

# Acknowledgments

Cover & frontis photograph ~ Ralph Wahl
Electronic pre-press ~ Marcus Yearout
Foreword ~ Bob Barnes
Improved spinning block ~ Jack Salstrom
Supplemental darkroom work ~ Quicksilver
Creative Consultant ~ Diane Van Demark
Special thanks to ~ Curt Kraemer, Biologist
Washington State Department Fish and Wildlife

## Photographs
Ralph Wahl
Fly tying, casting sequence
and color photography
D.B. Homel

Illustrations by the author

**On the cover and frontis** ~ Author Van Demark using the dry line method for spring steelhead on the Skagit River.

This book is dedicated to
a man named Don
who stirred my interest
and got me started . . .
a long time ago

# Table of Contents

# *Foreword*

For almost twenty years now it has been both my pleasure and travail to know and fish with Dick Van Demark. A pleasure because he brings a special zest and insight and a touch of whimsy to his companionship which transforms to commonplace into the extra special. A travail because his intensity can be uncomfortable at times as he challenges himself and his companions to discard the trappings of the pedantic and to probe ever deeper into the mores of the sport of angling - and to explore our understanding of why fish do what they do. His is a restless and an inquisitive spirit, always seeking out in the new explanations of the old, forever forging new theories as his experiences lead him to reject the old. But Dick is far more than a mere theoretician; he brings to his angling a blend of considerable fly tying skills, angling tactics, artistic understanding and perceptions of his quarry and the environment in which he chooses to pursue it that most of us can only hope to aspire to. His skills and understanding are drawn from what would be for many of us several lifetimes of angling experiences and intimate associations with a wide variety of waters and conditions.

Dick's flat-winged low water steelhead flies are very effective, however a word of caution may be in order. Having fished alongside Dick I can attest, as can many others, that his success with taking steelhead on a fly far transcends the mere lure that he uses. Had not A.H.E. Wood created the red and blue shank low water flies for atlantic salmon I am confident that Dick would have independently developed something very similar for steelhead and made us believers too. In fact, I have long secretly suspected that it was Dick in an earlier life who prompted Ed Zern's anecdote in *To Hell With Fishing*, about one Gollup Kuhn who caught a smallmouth bass by trolling a privy-door hinge in the Delaware River. Fortunately Dick is generous in both spirit and deed. In these pages he shares with us the distillation of his fly tying philosophy for successful steelhead flies developed over twenty years. He would, I assure you, ask that you read it and accept it only as one angler's philosophy and that you would in his spirit try it, challenge it and change it to meld it into your own fishing as your abilities and experiences so dictate.

Bob Barnes
Bellevue, Washington

# *Preface*

In pondering the many variables and unknowns of angling, most fly fishers I've known seem to be led naturally and inevitably to theorize about things they observe. Given enough time, many of us feel a compulsion to share with others our gleanings and ideas from many years in the game. Ergo, another book is born to adorn the ever-growing shelf of already existing titles. This book, my first, is a result of such a compulsion. It introduces a novel and effective series of low-water fly patterns for steelhead. It also endeavors to shed some different slants of light on fly design and discusses my approach to steelhead fly fishing.

Several years ago, Trey Combs contacted me about a book he was writing. He asked that I develop a chapter about my series of flat-winged low water steelhead flies. I gladly obliged this request and sent him a typed manuscript. A portion of that material was later incorporated, by paraphrase, into Trey's fine 1990 book, <u>Steelhead Fly Fishing</u>.

Over the intervening years, I added to my original writings and gave several copies of the enlarged manuscript to friends and acquaintances. Their responses, and the responses of those with whom they shared the manuscript, made it evident that there existed considerable interest in the work.

This book represents a substantial expansion and revision of the original "homemade" text and illustrations. It also includes the beautiful Ralph Wahl photographs.

My wish is that the reader will critically examine the contents, experiment with some of the ideas and fly patterns, and expand upon them. If this book achieves the objective of *complementing* the reader's understanding and adding something of worth to the long-standing, venerable sport of low-water fly fishing — it will have been well worth the effort involved.

Enjoy!

R. Van Demark
York District
Bellingham, Washington
August, 1995

# *Moving Water and the Dry Line*

In the final chapter of <u>A River Never Sleeps</u>, Roderick Haig Brown wrote of the essence of his love for rivers. Certain excerpts from this immortal testament stand out in my mind and summate with unparalleled beauty and eloquence my almost religious kinship to rivers:

> "A river is water in it's loveliest form ... knowing a river intimately is a very large part of the joy of fly fishing ... the full riches of discovery are not immediately released, they cannot be; only knowledge and close experience can release them ... If it were not for the strong, quick life of rivers ... I would fish less often."

And as Haig Brown writes; "perhaps fishing is, for me, only an excuse to be near rivers."

I've essentially remained a Northwesterner with neither the desire nor fantasy beliefs to take me to the far-flung or exotic waters of the world. Like the steelhead and the sea run cutthroat, I've tended to be a coastal-ranging creature with periodic migrations inland. Over the years my angling peregrinations have taken me to waters from northern California to northern British Columbia and as far inland as Montana; but never more than a drive of a day or so from my cherished Pacific Northwest.

My pursuit of steelhead with the fly has embraced many of Washington's rivers and several streams in British Columbia: Sol Duc, Columbia, Methow, Dean, Coquihalla, Elwha, Morice-Bulkley, Skagit, Klickatat, Thompson, Similkameen, Kalama, Lewis, Wenatchee, Toutle (before the St. Helens "blow-out"), Nooksack, Cascade, and my home river, the beloved Stillaguamish, are some of the waters that come to mind. Oregon's Deschutes and it's free-rising steelhead also evoke pleasant memories. There are other waters I prefer not to identify for they are off the beaten track and, as yet, relatively unknown. All have been good to me to various degrees . . . some frugal, some generous, and others profligate on occasion.

Moving waters hold the greatest fascination for me regardless of what species they may hold. No doubt, steelhead would hold less attraction for me where they not fish of the moving water, with it's endless complexities and the challenges it places on the angler. I do know of a lake which holds summer steelhead during late summer and early autumn. While it has produced well, I've fished it seldom since the "newness" wore off. A steelhead in still water seems to me to be just another rainbow trout, and I can go to some incredibly beautiful lakes in British Columbia whenever my wish is to fly fish for large rainbows in still water.

My preference as a steelhead fly fisher is the use of the dry line and flies fished in or on the surface. Even when conditions demand the sunken wet fly, I prefer the visual contact a dry line provides. Over the years, through a mixed process of my own innovations married to information provided by other anglers, I've more-or-less mastered special techniques and presentations which allow me to use the dry line most of the time; not only for steelhead, but for resident trout and other species as well.

When all my angling biases are added up, there is no fish response as exciting as an in-surface or on-the-surface take. As a result, much of my tackle tinkering and fly tying experimentation over the past few decades has been dedicated to this end—which leads to the discussion of how the *flat-winged* style of low water fly came to be.

*Author and steelhead locked in battle. (R. Wahl photo)*

# *Evolution of the*
## *Flat Winged Low-Water Fly Series*

Some years ago, I became increasingly bothered by the fact that nearly all of the low-water and dry fly steelhead patterns commonly used in the Northwest were of English, Canadian Maritime, or U.S. east coast origin or were slightly camouflaged modifications of such patterns. Patterns such as Blue Charm, Lady Caroline, Ackroyd, et al, produced and produced well, no question, and a few of these flies still occupy niches in one of my fly boxes.

Logic and the need for a local tradition seemed, in my mind, to demand distinct low-water and dry patterns of purely Northwest origin. This mild obsession continued for a time and was eventually converted in to action and reality.

My early attempts at "revolution" resulted in some productive low-water and dry fly patterns, but those initial attempts lacked the quality of distinctiveness I was looking for.

Then, in 1973, Pete Hidy described to me, in conversation, the special dubbing techniques conceived by he and Jim

Leisenring in the development of the flymph emerger patterns. Later a close friend, angling author/entomologist Rick Hafele, actually demonstrated the method to me with vise, spinning block, and thread at hand.

It did not require an Einsteinian leap of the mind for me to see the potential of applying the flymph dubbing method to steelhead flies, specifically low-water patterns. A few more months of thinking and experimenting from the fishes point-of-view, or more accurately the fishes' point of *viewing*, and all the ingredients were in place. I'd arrived at a low water dressing rationale that departed from east coast and English tradition in a number of characteristics. The rational has proved to be very productive. Moreover, these dressings have pleased me in terms of being aesthetically satisfying, while also fitting my criteria of how a low-water fly should function in the river, and how it should appear to the fish.

As I write about my creation, I do so with the knowledge that an angler or anglers living somewhere else, and unknown to me, may have arrived at a dressing style similar to my flat-winged low-water steelhead flies. My many decades in the sport have taught me several things, one of which I call the *convergent evolution principle of fly development*, which can be simply stated:

> As the materials and technology become available, several competent, creative anglers will solve an angling problem or conceive of inno-

vations in essentially similar ways at about the same time.

With that caveat established, I'll describe the salients of my approach to dressing low-water patterns. (Editor's note: Many of these vital principles of good fly design are also applicable to the construction of fly types for other species; i.e. trout nymphs, soft-hackles, streamers, salmon flies, sub-surface bass flies etc.)

## MOTILITY

The tying material used, particularly the body dressing and the hackle, should provide abundant movement when the fly is in the water. The long fibered hackles of game bird body feathers undulate and sway in the current; the uplifted, brushed floss tail ripples and moves in different directions according to the vagaries of the current; the fur fibers of the spun body project at many different angles and are in constant movement; and the soft body feather wings expand and contract. I dress all my in-surface and sub-surface flies with the idea of creating an underwater "aerobics show" for the fish. I rate motility high on the list of necessary attributes regardless of the species for which I'm creating a fly.

## REFRACTIVE QUALITY

From the fishes' point of view, any fly not fished on or near the bottom will be subject to the effects of multiple light sources such as; (1) direct overhead skylight, (2) refracted oblique light, (3) light reflected from the stream bottom and river banks, particulate matter in the water, and from trees and other objects on the shore. It follows, then, that translucent body materials with good refractive characteristics create a distinct advantage. In the case of the low-water fly which is viewed for the most part against direct skylight, the use of refractive materials is crucial. The spun fur, flymph type bodies of my low-water patterns provide an abundance of refraction. All patterns in the series utilize translucent materials. Seal fur (now banned and rightly so), Seal-Ex (a seal substitute), Antron, mohair goat, and Kodel polyester yarn (chopped-up and run through a blender) are all appropriate materials with good refractive qualities; but if dubbed too tightly or heavily will lose much of their luster. Stated another way, the refractive qualities of these materials are brought to best effect by using them rather sparsely—and then spinning them on waxed silk (or in a dubbing loop) which results in the fibers projecting at many different angles to bend and disperse both indirect and local light in many directions.

## OPTICAL BLENDING

I have long believed, as have many other fly dressers, that dubbing with a mix of two or more colors, shades, or tints is much more effective than dubbing a single, solid color. Being an artist, as well as an angler, I've brought some basic artistic principles into play in my choice of colors for patterns in this series through the principles of *optical blending* and *simultaneous contrast*. Simply stated, an optical blend works as follows:

> Two or more colors of hair or fur, red and yellow for example, when mixed will appear at a distance as orange, yellow-orange, or red-orange depending on the relative proportions of red and yellow used in the mix. However, as the optically blended mass is approached closely, the component colors rather suddenly become discernible and vivid.

I believe that as a fish closes in on a fly with an optically blended body, the rapidly changing color effects must excite the fish's sensory receptors very much and result in a higher percentage of "takes". The details of optical blending are discussed further in the next chapter.

The bodies of all patterns in my low water series employ optical blending. One pattern, *The Royal Blue*, also uses the principle of simultaneous contrast through the use of the complementary colors blue and orange, in a half-and-half body. To explain, complementary colors exist opposite each other on a standard color wheel - red and green, yellow and violet, blue and orange, yellow-green and red-violet, and so forth. Whenever such colors are juxtaposed, both will be greatly intensified because of their mutual and simultaneous contrast. Dressings employing this principle tend to be very visible under all light conditions. Not surprisingly, my Royal Blue pattern is particularly effective under low light conditions such as heavy shade, overcast days, at dawn and twilight, and also in slightly off-colored water.

## USE OF A FLAT WING

All patterns in this series are dressed flat winged. This is again a concession to the fish's perspective from below the fly. Body feathers from various sources (golden pheasant, grouse, duck) are used because of their relative translucency and the tendency of their fibers to be constantly in motion when in a current. The flat wing under-girded by a few stiff hairs also serves as a planing surface when the riffle-hitch method of presentation is used.

## COLOR INTENSITY

The well worn adage about muted patterns for bright conditions and more intensely contrasted or colorful patterns under lower light conditions is more than just fanciful thinking. My series of low water patterns quite intentionally includes a range of color intensities to cover most light conditions.

## SILK AND FLOSS

I select a dubbing silk color that will either enhance or be neutral with respect to the colors used in the dubbing mix— depending on the degree of intensity or muteness desired.

The use of a fluorescent floss tail for "attractor purposes" (i.e. attraction at a distance) is another distinguishing characteristic of my low water fly series. The tail color matches the color of the floss in the tag.

# Optical Blending and Color

In mixing paint; paints of different colors, tints, and shades are directly mixed to create a different and homogeneous hue and/or value. This is not possible with fur or hair, obviously, so a method involving sensory illusion must be used.

Optical blending is based on the phenomena that the eye is unable to distinguish juxtaposed colors at a distance, if the color objects are very thin or small. You can conduct a simple drawing experiment to demonstrate optical blending for yourself:

Use a ruler and draw a series of thin lines very close together alternating blue, orange, blue, orange and so on. Now step back a few paces and you will see that your orange and blue field has become gray. Move toward your color field slowly and notice that at a certain point you will rather abruptly see the alternating blue and orange lines return. It is probable that the same thing happens as a fish approaches an optically blended fly. A number of experiments have demonstrated that many types of fish, including trout, are able to perceive the entire visible spectrum. Fish can also see into the infrared and ultraviolet ranges on either side of the visible spectrum as well. Other experiments have shown that trout can discern minute detail at close viewing distances.

So it is with optically blended dubbing. The individual fur fibers are very thin but discrete filaments (analogous to the lines of the optical blending experiment). Thus, fur mixes of different hues and intensities will appear quite different at a distance, but will resolve into component colors suddenly on closer approach. As I stated earlier, I believe this must be very stimulating to a fish's visual sensors and will cause approach much more often than avoidance (i.e. "spooking" or refusal).

The dubbing mix used in my *Optical Black* low water pattern provides a somewhat spectacular example of the visual effects of optical blending. The mix consists of equal parts dark green, dark blue, crimson, and dark gray (or black). At a distance, the dubbed body appears dark gray with a light twinkling at the ends of the projecting fibers - and sometimes a halo effect. Upon closer approach against a background of light, the mixture not only breaks into it's component colors, but also a myriad of intermediate colors—blue greens, red violets, blue violets, etc., as a result of refraction through the translucent furs used and consequent reinforcement or cancellation of light waves.

*Large British Columbia steelhead seduced by a Mai Tai flat winged fly. (D. Van Demark photo)*

*Looking downstream at the famous "Elbow Hole", North Fork Stillaguamish River in Washington State. (R. Wahl photo)*

# *An Experiment*

Some years ago, I conducted a simple experiment on several occasions—to wit; alternately fishing two dry flies identical in every aspect but the dubbing. One fly had a black fur dubbed body (hereinafter referred to as the "SBB fly", denoting a solid black body), while the other fly had a blended body in which black fur was muted by adding an equal amount of medium brown fur (hereinafter referred to as the "BB fly", denoting blended body). Black was chosen because of it's high contrast and intensity; medium brown because of it's quality of toning down intensity and it's low contrast relative to black.

In each trial, the flies were alternately fished for equal amounts of time—the "SBB fly" for a half hour, the "BB fly" for a half hour, and so on until that day's trial was over. Each trial in a given series was restricted to the same stretch of river. The other requisites were:

(1) That there be enough steelhead in the stream to obviate blind chance as a significant factor.

(2) That the water be clear.

(3) And, that I be fishing alone during all trials in as much that the immediate presence of a companion angler would have constituted an uncontrollable variable.

Trials were conducted at different times of the day with several trials for any given time interval. The experiment involved summer steelhead.

Both flies were tied in modified Wulff style with wings spread at an angle of thirty degrees (cocked forward slightly), and the bottoms were clipped short so the fly would ride low in the water. The dressings were:

| | |
|---|---|
| **Tail** | Natural grayish-brown deer body hair |
| **Body** | Solid black fur body (SBB), or Equal parts of black and medium brown fur thoroughly blended (BB) |
| **Hackle** | Mixed hackle of grizzly and iron blue dun with bottom fibers clipped to a length equal to the hook's gap |
| **Wings** | Natural grayish-brown deer body hair tied as described above |

All flies used were tied on size 6 Partridge *Wilson* single dry fly hooks. Hooks were debarbed.

My underlying hypothesis was that, overall, flies with very intense, high contrast bodies would not produce as well as flies having less intensity and contrast under summer conditions of low, clear water. My criterion for productivity was the number of solid takes by steelhead.

The experiment was conducted over a period of two years during the months of July through September, and demonstrated two important things:

> (A) Under very low light conditions there was not a consequential difference in the takes-per-unit-of-effort between the "SBB fly" and the "BB fly".
>
> (B) Under bright light conditions, the "BB flies" out-performed the "SBB flies" by a significant margin. The takes-per-unit-of-effort ratio of the BB vs. SBB fly was greater than two to one. In some trials, under very bright conditions, the ratio approached three to one.

Others, of course, may make of this what they want. My object in these trials was to prove or disapprove a personal hypothesis to satisfy my own curiosity alone.

I have often heard steelhead fly fishers voice the maxim: "Where steelhead flies are concerned, I agree with Henry Ford - give me any color as long as it's black"! Under discolored water conditions, high water run-off, and very low light levels they may have a point. I believe, however, that this well-worn and over used precept rests on very shaky ground when purported as a "truth" generally applicable to all or even a majority of steelheading conditions.

*Beautiful Skeena hen, eighteen pounds plus, taken on the Dark Ale (D. Van Demark photo)*

**THE FLAT WINGED LOW WATER SERIES**
(top to bottom)
**Left Row:** *Creme De Menthe, Bright Sienna, Blood 'N Brandy.*
**Right Row:** *Dark Priest, Maulin Rouge, and Dark Ale.*

**THE FLAT WINGED LOW WATER SERIES**
(top to bottom)
**Left Row:** *Royal Blue, Brazen Lady, Mai Tai.*
**Right Row:** *Optical Black, Tawney Port, and Low Water Bee.*

**WING AND HACKLE MATERIALS**
(See page 126 for complete description)

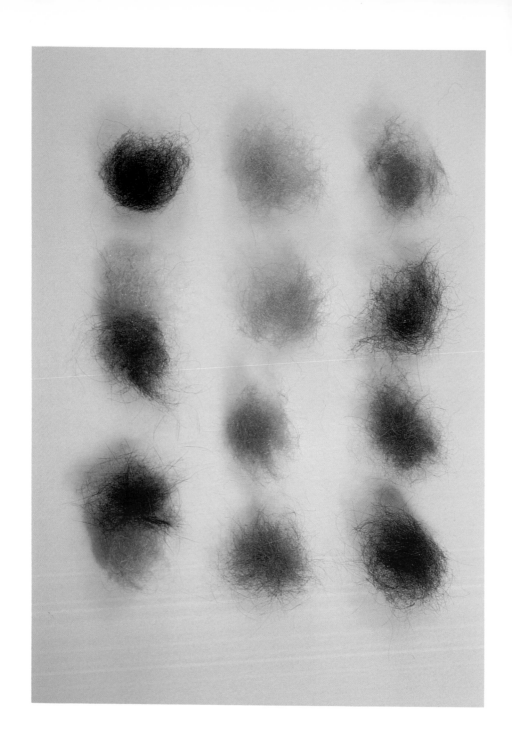

**BLENDED DUBBING**
(See page 126 for identification)

# Fly Patterns

## The Flat-Winged Low Water Series

## BLOOD 'N BRANDY

Tying thread ~ flame or red

Tip ~ gold mylar

Tag ~ gold mylar overwrapped with fluorescent flame floss

Tail ~ 4 or 5 strands of flame floss, clipped short and brushed

Body ~ dubbing mix of 3 parts hot orange, 1 part fluorescent yellow and 1 or 2 parts scarlet (depending on the degree of "red-orangeness" desired)

Dubbing silk ~ orange or red

Ribbing ~ gold rope

Hackle ~ gray and white flank feathers from a mallard or teal drake dyed hot orange

Underwing ~ a few fibers of red hair

Overwing ~ two golden pheasant tippets dyed scarlet

## BRAZEN LADY

Tying thread ~ flame or dark brown
Tip ~ silver mylar
Tag ~ silver mylar overwrapped with fluorescent flame
    floss
Tail ~ 4 or 5 strands of flame floss
Body ~ copper tinsel yarn, preferred; copper tinsel may
    be substituted
Dubbing silk ~ not applicable
Ribbing ~ none
Hackle ~ reddish orange golden pheasant body feather
Underwing ~ a few fibers of red hair
Overwing ~ two ruddy brown shoulder feathers from
    wing of golden pheasant

## BRIGHT SIENNA

Tying thread ~ brown
Tip ~ gold mylar
Tag ~ gold mylar overwrapped with fluorescent yellow-
    orange floss
Tail ~ 4 or 5 strands of fluorescent yellow-orange floss
Body ~ dubbing mix of 2 parts burnt sienna (vivid
    reddish brown) and 1 part hot orange
Dubbing silk ~ orange or yellow
Ribbing ~ gold rope
Hackle ~ reddish orange golden pheasant body feather
Underwing ~ a few fibers of yellow hair
Overwing ~ two ruddy brown shoulder feathers from
    wing of golden pheasant

## CREME-DE-MENTHE

Tying thread ~ olive
Tip ~ gold mylar
Tag ~ gold mylar overwrapped with fluorescent yellow-
     orange floss
Tail ~ 4 or 5 strands of fluorescent yellow-orange floss
Body ~ dubbing mix of 3 parts dark olive and 2 parts lime
     (chartreuse)
Dubbing silk ~ yellow or olive
Ribbing ~ gold rope
Hackle ~ greenish gray feather from Chinese cock
     pheasant rump
Underwing ~ a few fibers of light yellow or white hair
Overwing ~ two greenish gray feathers from Chinese
     cock pheasant rump

## DARK ALE

Tying thread ~ brown
Tip ~ gold mylar
Tag ~ gold mylar overwrapped with fluorescent salmon
     orange floss
Tail ~ 4 or 5 strands of fluorescent salmon orange floss
Body ~ dubbing mix of 2 parts dark brown and 1 part
     maroon
Dubbing silk ~ orange
Ribbing ~ gold rope
Hackle ~ long fibered English grouse body feather or
     merganser flank feather
Underwing ~ a few fibers of orange hair
Overwing ~ two reddish orange golden pheasant body
     feathers

## LOW WATER BEE

Tying thread ~ brown
Tip ~ gold mylar
Tag ~ gold mylar overwrapped with fluorescent yellow-
    orange floss
Tail ~ 4 or 5 strands of bright red floss
Body ~ medium brown, yellow band, medium brown (the
    yellow center band is a mix of 1 part fluorescent
    yellow and 1 part regular yellow)
Dubbing silk ~ brown or yellow
Ribbing ~ none
Hackle ~ brownish Chinese cock pheasant rump
Underwing ~ a few fibers of red hair
Overwing ~ two brownish partridge feathers with cream
    center stripe from trailing edge of male
    Hungarian partridge wing

## MAI TAI

Tying silk ~ red
Tip ~ silver mylar
Tag ~ silver mylar overwrapped with fluorescent yellow-
    orange floss
Tail ~ 4 or 5 strands of fluorescent yellow-orange floss
Body ~ dubbing mix of 2 parts hot orange, 3 parts scarlet,
    and 2 parts maroon
Dubbing silk ~ orange or red
Ribbing ~ silver rope
Hackle ~ Chinese cock rump feather dyed red which
    results in a maroon color
Underwing ~ a few fibers of orange hair
Overwing ~ two brownish partridge feathers with cream
    center stripe from the trailing edge of male
    Hungarian partridge wing

## MOULIN ROUGE
Tying silk ~ flame or red
Tip ~ gold mylar
Tag ~ gold mylar overwrapped with fluorescent flame
    floss
Tail ~ 4 or 5 strands of fluorescent flame floss
Body ~ dubbing mix of equal parts scarlet and
    fluorescent orange
Dubbing silk ~ orange or red
Ribbing ~ gold rope
Hackle ~ greenish gray Chinese cock pheasant rump
    feather
Underwing ~ a few fibers of red hair
Overwing ~ two reddish orange golden pheasant body
    feathers


## OPTICAL BLACK
Tying thread ~ black
Tip ~ silver mylar
Tag ~ silver mylar overwrapped with fluorescent
    salmon orange floss
Tail ~ 4 or 5 strands of fluorescent salmon orange floss
Body ~ dubbing mix of equal parts dark blue, crimson,
    dark green, and dark gray or black
Dubbing silk ~ purple or red
Ribbing ~ silver rope
Hackle ~ reddish orange body feather from golden
    pheasant
Underwing ~ a few fibers of red hair
Overwing ~ two ruddy brown shoulder feathers from
    wing of golden pheasant

## ROYAL BLUE

Tying thread ~ black
Tip ~ silver mylar
Tag ~ silver mylar
Tail ~ fibers from feather dyed "Rit" royal blue
Body ~ rear half dubbing dyed "Rit" royal blue; front half
      dubbing mix 1 part fluorescent yellow and 2 parts
      fluorescent scarlet
Dubbing silk ~ orange
Ribbing ~ silver rope, rear half only
Hackle ~ gray and white flank feathers from mallard or
      teal drake dyed royal blue
Underwing ~ not more than 6 strands of silver
        "Flashabou" clipped even with tag
Overwing ~ two gray and white mallard drake body
      feathers dyed fluorescent scarlet


## TAWNY PORT

Tying thread ~ red
Tip ~ gold mylar
Tag ~ gold mylar overwrapped with fluorescent salmon
      orange floss
Tail ~ 4 or 5 strands of fluorescent salmon orange floss
Body ~ dubbing mix of 2 parts hot orange and 3 parts
      maroon
Dubbing silk ~ red or orange
Ribbing ~ gold rope
Hackle ~ reddish orange golden pheasant body feather
Underwing ~ a few fibers of yellow or golden hair
Overwing ~ two golden pheasant tippet feathers

## DARK PRIEST

Tying thread ~ black or brown
Tip ~ gold mylar
Tag ~ gold mylar overwrapped with fluorescent yellow-
orange floss
Tail ~ 4 or 5 strands of fluorescent yellow-orange floss
Body ~ dubbing mix of 2 parts black, 2 parts medium
brown, and 1 part maroon
Dubbing silk ~ black or brown
Ribbing ~ gold rope
Hackle ~ Chinese cock pheasant rump feather dyed black
Underwing ~ a few fibers of orange hair
Overwing ~ two well marked brown English grouse
body feathers

# *Additional Tying Notes*

**(1)** The fluorescent floss used in the tag and tail for most of the series is Danville's Depth Ray Floss. In those patterns calling for *yellow-orange* floss, the floss used is 1X Super Floss, color #600 (rust orange), distributed by Uni Products of Canada.

**(2)** For the ribbing rope, I highly recommend a French product available in both silver and gold: DMC Fil d'Or a Broder (gold) and Fil d'Argent a Broder (silver), size 10, on a 60 meter spool. The manufacturer is Dollfus-Mieg & Cie—Paris. It is available through fine domestic sewing shops.

**(3)** It is very important to use a highly translucent fur for the dubbed bodies of this series (or synthetic substitutes such as "Seal-Ex") due to the ability of these materials to strongly refract light. Mohair goat is a quite translucent natural fur and when mixed with Antron (tri-lobal nylon) fibers is a convincing seal substitute. Both materials tend to be long fibered and should be chopped-up before blending. The least expensive alternative is to use synthetic, translucent yarns chopped-up irregularly with a scissors and then run through a blender. Appropriate synthetic yarns include:

100% unspun Kodel Polyester knitting yarn
Dawn Odyssey yarn by American Thread Co.
Aunt Lydia's heavy rug yarn by ATC
Aunt Lydia's worsted weight acrylic yarn

In fact, just about any synthetic yarn made of acrylic, polyester, or antron fibers will do provided it is color-fast and of knitting weight.

**(4)** My original dubbing mixes given in the foregoing pattern dressings were based on the use of pre-embargo seal fur. These original formulas will not give the same color effects when synthetic and/or natural fibers other than seal are utilized. Thus adjustments in the formula proportions are necessary. *See appendix for a listing of equivalent mixes derived by the author for each pattern in the series.*

*The author in his fly tying room (D.B. Homel photo)*

*The "Turkey Shoot", Grand Ronde River  (R. Wahl photo)*

# Dressing the
## flat winged low-water fly

The following instructions and drawings represent a detailed description of the 15 steps necessary to dress the flat winged low water steelhead fly.

## A NOTE ABOUT HOOKS

For reasons of tradition and aesthetics, I prefer classic atlantic salmon fly hooks. The Tiemco TMC 7989 is a well made hook, and quite expensive. It can be used for either dry flies of low water fly patterns. Mustad's #90240 low water salmon hook has a short, hollow point, is adequate, and costs quite a bit less than the TMC. My favorite hook is the Partridge single *Wilson* dry fly hook. It works equally well when used as a low water hook. The Wilson has an extremely beautiful shape and is of high quality. It is costlier than the Mustad and less expensive than the Tiemco.

## TYING INSTRUCTIONS

**(1)**  Wrap tying thread from eye of hook to point shown, then wrap forward approximately 3/16 inch.  Tie off with a half-hitch.

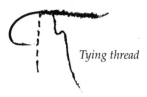

Tying thread

**(2)**  Tie in a piece of size 14 flat mylar tinsel tapered with scissors at the end to be tied in.  Wrap back to the end of tying-thread-covered portion of the shank, then wrap forward to the starting point—thus creating a double mylar wrap (which is more durable and neater than a single wrap).

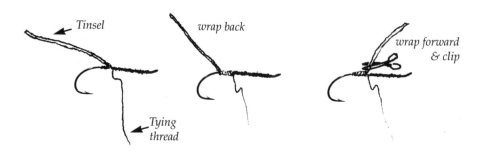

Tinsel
wrap back
wrap forward & clip
Tying thread

**(3)**  Tie in a piece of fluorescent floss and wrap back to a position where 2/3rds of the mylar is covered (thus leaving a tinsel tip), then wrap forward to starting point. Tie off and clip excess floss. You have just formed a floss *tag* . There is a very important reason for wrapping the floss over the tinsel. When in the water, the light is reflected from the tinsel under-layer which causes the floss to literally glow with intense color. Conversely, if the floss were wrapped over most tying thread, it would be greatly dulled and rendered nearly useless as a fish attractor.

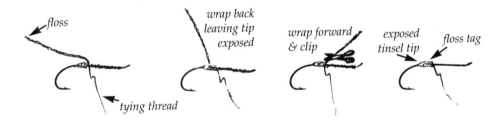

**(4)** Tie in 4 or 5 strands of fluorescent floss to make the tail (same color as the floss used to make the tag.) Then take a reverse loop behind the tail bringing the tying thread back over the shank in front of the tail. With the thread in this position hold the tail with left thumb and forefinger—and tighten the loop by pulling the tying thread down on the far side of the shank. This will lift the tail. Clear as a polluted pond? Hopefully the diagrams will help.

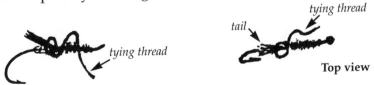

Tie off the tail with a half-hitch, then clip it short (about twice the length of the tag and tip). Finally, brush out the tail with a fine comb, Velcro, or anything suited to the task.

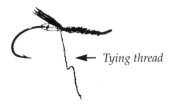

Tying thread

**(5)** Tie in a piece of medium tinsel rope on the underside of the hook shank. You may find it convenient to invert the hook to do this. Return the hook to the normal upright position in the vise and tie in a pre-made spun fur body made as described in the section on use of a spinning block (see appendix). Wind tying thread to a point 1/8 to 3/16 of an inch behind the eye of the hook.

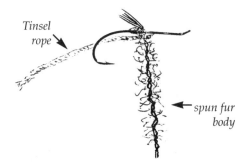

Tinsel rope

spun fur body

**(6)** Wind on the spun fur body and tie off. Counterwind with the tinsel rope and tie off again with a half-hitch. Rough up the body a bit at this point by stroking it with a small piece of Velcro glued to the end of a popsicle stick.

← *Tying thread*

## OPTIONAL METHOD FOR MAKING BODY

Make a *dubbing loop* from the tying thread by doubling it and then wrapping it down on the hook shank. Next, wrap the tying thread forward to just behind the hook eye.

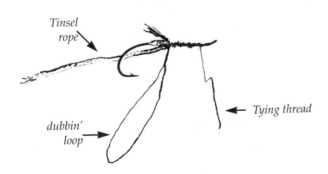

*Tinsel rope*

*dubbin' loop* →

← *Tying thread*

Insert the dubbing fur between the two strands of the loop and twist by twirling a spinning tool (commercially made or homemade from a paper clip), clockwise until you have a moderately tight, spun fur body.

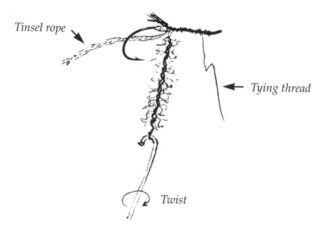

*Tinsel rope*

*Tying thread*

*Twist*

Proceed to wrap-on the fur body and counter-wrap with tinsel rope the same as in steps 5 and 6.

**NOTE** - Though the optional method is some-what faster, the spinning block method allows a more even spread of the dubbing fur and enables the tyer to position the fur at right angles to the thread. With a little practice, you'll find that the spinning block yields far better tying results.

**(7)** Prepare a body feather (for the *hackle* ) with fibers of sufficient length to reach the hook point or somewhat beyond. [A] Stroke hackle fibers to be at more or less right angles to the shaft of the feather. [B] Clip a few fibers from both sides of the stem very short. The fibers on the side of the stem which will be down when tied in (right side as you view the feather convex side up) should be clipped about 3/16 inch further than the fibers on the left side of the stem. This little tying trick has the result of making the feather lay right as you begin winding the hackle—greatly easing the task, particularly when working with body and flank feathers.

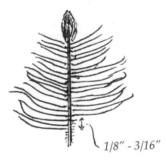

1/8" - 3/16"

**(8)** Crimp the clipped stem between your thumb and forefinger. Tie in about 1/4 turn down the circumference of the hook (facing you).

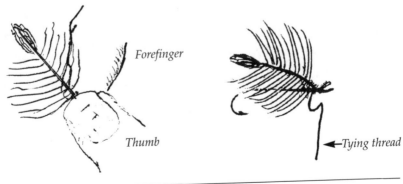

Forefinger

Thumb

←Tying thread

**(9)** Attach hackle pliers to tip of hackle feather, pull straight up, and fold the feather by gently stroking fibers on both sides of the stem toward the rear with your thumb, forefinger, and middle finger. (Helpful hint—moistening your fingers will make the feather folding process much easier.)

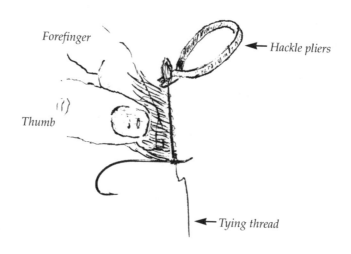

Forefinger

Hackle pliers

Thumb

Tying thread

**(10)** Continue to hold the folded fibers as you make the first 1/3 to 1/2 turn, then let go. The fibers will usually, but not always, stay oriented once the feather has been wound against and part way around the hook shank. Sometimes a second stroking of the fibers is necessary as the hackle is brought down and under the hook shank. Complete one full turn (or, at most two) and tie-off with a half-hitch. The flies in this series are designed to be dressed sparsely in the hackle.

**(11)** Clip off all top hackle fibers.

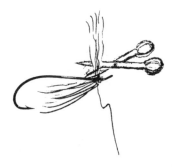

**(12)** Tie in a <u>few hairs</u>, 1/2 to 3/4 body length to lend support to the wings which will be applied in the next step. The hairs are the *underwing*. The hairs will also enhance the color of the wings. These hairs are to be spread out on the top of and slightly down the shank, not tied in as a clump.

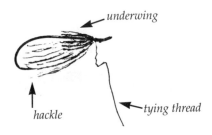

**(13)** Prepare two matched body feathers. <u>Do</u> <u>not</u> use feathers with a pronounced curve in the stem. A slight curve is desirable, however.

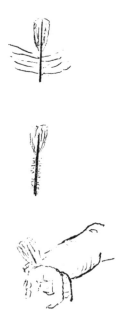

[a] Stroke lower fibers down, leaving a solid wing section the length of the fly's body, excluding the tag and tip (or slightly shorter).

[b] Clip the stroked-out fibers close to the stem on both sides.

[c] Crimp stem between thumb and forefinger where stubble meets wing.

**(14)** Tie in body feathers flat, one at a time, and align one on top of the other. This forms the *overwing*. Clip off excess stems.

**(15)** Build a neat head with the tying thread, whip finish, and coat with fly head cement.

Congratulations, you have just successfully tied a flat winged low water fly!

**NOTES**:
The flies pictured in this book were made with conventional sized heads for aesthetic purposes. In tying low water flies for use on the steelhead stream, I leave space during the tying operation for a longer than normal head. The long head provides space for the use of a Portland or riffle-hitch knot which I occasionally employ.

Dubbing formulas given in the fly pattern chapter which follows, presume use of dyed animal furs. Equivalent *synthetic* dubbing formulas are listed in Appendix 2.

*The "747 Pool", North Fork Stillaguamish  (R. Wahl photo)*

# Fishing Conditions
# &
# Fly Selection

I've written this section to provide some general fly selection guidelines and a pattern rational for the flies of the low water series; and have done so with a degree of reticence knowing full well that categorization of pattern selection vis-a-vis fishing conditions has a large element of subjectivity and can be only approximate, at best.

There are always exceptions to such generalized schema. I know more than one angler who does quite well using only flies on the bright end of the fly dressing spectrum; conversely, I also know of other successful anglers who consistently use flies on the dark, intense contrast side.

Another reality is that other steelhead fly fishers, some of whom are internationally recognized, hold views divergent from mine—and no doubt have substantial basis for holding these views.

Thus I must stress the caveat that what follows are but one man's ideas, theories, and conclusions. However, hypothesizing and theorizing are at least half the fun of the game, aren't they? I also must qualify that what I have written here is based on my experiences and observations as a steelhead fly fisher of northwestern coastal and inland rivers. This information may or may not be applicable in other regions where anadromous salmonids are found.

Having covered my fanny, as it were, I'll get into the topic at hand.

The twelve patterns which make up this series provide a range of color intensities and hues that, collectively, are intended to cover the varying light conditions encountered in low water fishing. This perhaps could have been done with a series of, say, a half-dozen patterns; but having a wider option of patterns to select from, according to my streamside observations and "hunches", adds much enjoyment to my fishing.

I typically tie my low water patterns in sizes 4 and 6. I also carry a few flies in size 8 and even 10, as these small sizes will often produce in slow moving water and under extreme low water conditions when larger flies may be only marginally productive.

I have already implied my belief that there are few, if any, absolutes in the arena of steelhead fly fishing. But some decades of experience have led me to think that fish tend to react to certain types of visual stimuli better than others under a particular fishing condition.

In the three paragraphs that follow, I describe several rather broad-brush categories of low water fishing conditions and discuss my conclusions about the types of patterns summer steelhead prefer under each condition:

**(1)** Fish not long out of salt water and actively moving upriver (this occurs for the most part during the early to mid-summer period in my area) tend to respond to brightly hued flies or to flies which are dark and "contrasty". The same tendencies appear in late fall fish which are much closer to sexual maturity and are therefore more territorial and aggressive.

**(2)** With lower, warmer water conditions during the mid-summer and early fall period, fish are less active. At that time steelhead preferences shift to neutral intensity flies and flies of a dull, subdued cast. This is especially true when the light is on the water. My rule-of-thumb is . . . the brighter the light, the more subdued the fly.

**(3)** Fish show a preference for dark patterns under the low light conditions of late evening or a heavily overcast day. The very low light conditions of twilight and pre-dawn call for dark, intense contrast flies, particularly in the twilight period. Black is the most intense "dark" and it is only under extreme low light that I use pure black patterns. Otherwise, I prefer patterns in which I have "cut" (de-intensified) black with dubbings of less intensity, or use dark flies of other colors.

Having laid the framework, I'll bring some specificity to bear on each of the patterns in the steelhead low water series—based on my experiences and observations in using and testing these flies over the years. I have slipped in a few memorable fish stories involving flies of the series, and hope this will not be considered immodest. The stories are not intended as braggadocio, but rather to pique the reader's interest.

# *Bright Patterns*

## BLOOD 'N BRANDY

This is an early fly of the series which still ranks among my favorites. This fly could be considered taxonomically as a prawn pattern if one wishes to engage in this type of classification. Blood 'N Brandy has been a faithful producer of fresh summer run steelhead over many years and has exacted a heavy toll on autumn fish. Smaller sizes of this fly (#6 and #8) have, in several instances, taken fish during very low water conditions in mid-season, even under undiminished bright skies. When used in mid-season, it is at it's best after a heavy summer rainstorm has stimulated steelhead to begin moving actively.

## MOULIN ROUGE

Rain squalls moved up the valley of a medium sized British Columbia river as I worked my way down the chute of the pool toward a point where the bottom shelved diagonally on my side of the river. Moulin Rouge moved over the shelf just under the surface and then began slowly swinging with controlled drag. I was in the midst of thinking . . . "There should have been a take as the fly crossed the shelf", when the Rouge was picked-up by a fish going away in the most savage, crunching strike I had ever experienced. My reel began screaming almost instantly as I stood in awed amazement. Thirty minutes of grueling, brutal slugfest later, the fish lay quietly finning in the shallows at my feet calmly accepting her release. This magnificent twenty-pound-plus hen fish occupies a treasured place in my museum of angling memories as the largest summer run steelhead I have ever beached or, for that matter, am likely to beach in the future. The most highly colored fly of the series, Moulin Rouge, works especially well on fresh-run, moving fish and autumn fish. Oddly enough, in light of it's somewhat gaudy dress, the Rouge often does well under conditions where one would not choose a bright fly. I'm not certain why this is so.

# *Subdued Patterns*

### <u>LOW WATER BEE</u>

This pattern is my low water fly adaptation of Roderick Haig-Brown's celebrated Steelhead Bee dry fly. Like it's famous counterpart, the Low Water Bee has a way with summer steelhead. I frequently select this pattern during the mid-season, particularly when there is considerable light on the water. At times, I will knot this fly on in the morning and fish it until sundown has covered the water in shadow. Such is my faith in the Bee.

## CREME-DE-MENTHE

The Creme-de-Menthe pattern ranks equally high in my book for bright light work. I also have found it useful under somewhat diminished light conditions.

A few years back, I was working a boulder strewn run on an Olympic Peninsula stream, in early September, under a bright mid-afternoon sun. An almost imperceptible disturbance in the broken surface near the fly, caught my eye - and I tightened on the line more out of habit than anything else. The surface burst open and a large steelhead catapulted skyward with the Creme-de-Menthe solidly lodged in it's jaw. Nearly three-quarters of an hour later with my glands belting out large pumps of adrenaline, I was finally able to bring the fish to hand. I stood arm raised in respectful salute to the fish, sixteen pounds of silvery chrome beauty, as the remarkable battler swam slowly back to her station in the stream.

# Moderate Intensity Patterns

The four patterns that follow fall within a mid-range of hues and contrast. They are effective mid-season flies, and will also produce early and late in the season. For these reasons, I consider them to be the general purpose workhorses of the series.

## BURNT SIENNA

An intriguing pattern of an unusual hue, this fly is a later pattern in the series with but a few seasons under it's belt. During it's apprentice period, I used it somewhat sporadically. But, after a couple of seasons, it became evident that the steelhead of mid-season found this fly to their liking. I now fish this pattern with confidence. It may well become one of my favorite.

## TAWNY PORT

An old-timer in the series, I use the Tawny Port under moderate light conditions (high overcast, late afternoon and into evening) as a less intense alternative to darker, more highly contrasted patterns. It is a proven producer and, as implied, I use it as a role player.

Several memories are associated with this pattern. A particular memory stands out as I write this.

Some years ago, I was fishing a northern British Columbia river in early September. I fished the first three days under unbroken bluebird skies, releasing several steelhead that were mostly taken on dry flies. The fourth day I woke to a solid but high overcast sky as the remnant of a coastal storm moved through.

Mid-morning found me fishing the edge of some curving fast water above a vast three hundred meter long pool. After an hour of changing flies, my mind snapped to the realization that the situation was tailor-made for the Tawny Port. What happened during the next two hours was stuff of which angler's dreams are concocted: Seven takes, five steelhead solidly hooked, and three fish ranging from six to eleven pounds brought to the beach and released. Tawny Port had again proved it's mettle as a role player.

## MAI TAI

This pattern for no good reason languished, a wallflower in my fly box, for some time after I conceived it. Eventually, I gave the fly a fair trial and it became a belle-of-the-ball. As I set down these words, Mai Tai rests two feet in front of me in the jaws of a tying vise as both an inspiration and a reminder.

## DARK ALE

Close observation of this pattern will reveal that it is of low intensity darkness. This effect was purposefully created by use of a brown and maroon dubbing mix, the use of english grouse body feathers (with their soft browns and ochres), in addition to the soft peculiar red-orange glow of golden pheasant flank feathers.

I fish this pattern with confidence. It has taken several nice summer run steelhead. Need I say more?

# *Tinsel Body Flies*

Fully tinsel body flies are a puzzlement to me. I've found them to be productive at times and nearly worthless at others. They can produce under a variety of conditions provided there is enough light in the water to bring out their inherent reflective qualities—and they can be unproductive under the same range of conditions. I believe their "moodiness" may be related to the hard, stiff quality of the tinsel body, a characteristic which simply does <u>not</u> suggest life. I have included but one tinsel body pattern in the series, and have compensated for the immobile hardness of the body by incorporating a soft pheasant body feather with it's highly motile fibers to give the suggestion of life.

## <u>BRAZEN LADY</u>

Despite my earlier remonstrations, I would not be without at least one tinsel body pattern in my fly box when fishing the typical mid-season conditions of low water flows, bright light, and extreme water clarity.

Though I have a personal predilection for copper tinsel yarn because it is more subtle in it's reflection than glaring silver and gold tinsels, this pattern might well be equally effective with a gold or silver body.

The Brazen Lady has moved some difficult mid-season fish and has also scored early and late in the season. When it is effective, it can be very much so.

One instance which springs to mind occurred in the fall on a side channel of a British Columbia river where a considerable number of steelhead were holed-up below upstream shallows glutted with spawning humpback salmon. I fruitlessly worked these fish for the better part of a morning with a number of patterns, both low-water and dry. Then I removed Brazen Lady from her place in the fly box and threw her to the mercy of what had been a docile wolf pack. In short order, Brazen Lady seduced four steelhead. Would it be gilding the lily to say that three of the four were males?

# Dark Patterns

## OPTICAL BLACK

Here is one of the stars of the low water series. A mixture of several dubbings gives the illusion of dark gray or black when viewed from a distance through the phenomena of *optical blending* —thus the name, Optical Black.

Looked at more closely against a background of light, the multicolored translucent body fibers yield a kaleidoscope of colors through lightwave refraction.

This pattern has been particularly effective as a late afternoon and evening fly; and it produces on overcast days as well. It is one of my favorites.

Of the creditable number of steelhead which have succumbed to the Optical Black, a particular fish stands out in my mind. A henfish, this extraordinarily energetic summer-run took with a bold, splashy show. After two runs deep into the backing, several shorter sprints, and an amazing seventeen leaps clear of the water, I returned the twelve plus pound bundle of stamina back to her waters.

I stood on the beach for a very long while, my body drained and trembling, reliving the entire astonishing battle.


## ROYAL BLUE

I tie two versions of this pattern: One having a silver Flashabou underwing extending well beyond the flat tied overwings; the other having an underwing of a few short fibers of red hair. Both versions are effective, but the first has, for me, proved outstanding in the late evening and under gray sky conditions; therefore I'll focus on it.

Some may ask, "Why place the Flashabou as an underwing?" This is a fair question and I will endeavor to answer it.

In flowing waters, the slight curvature of the body feather overwings act like a foil, creating considerable turbulence which causes the thin Flashabou strips to undulate vigorously. This movement not only simulates life, but also sends out a high amount of vibrating flash which has, in my experience, proved very stimulating to steelhead. An aeronautical engineer could, no doubt, provide a far more coherent description of the phenomenon. I arrived at the design intuitively rather than by conscious application of engineering principles.

I recall an early October fishing trip to an inland river (a tributary of the Columbia) some years ago. The area had experienced a drought which had lasted most of the summer and into the fall. Arriving at the river, I plunged into immediate despair, for the water level was as low as I'd ever seen it. Daytime water temperatures were soaring into the high 60's. As a result, the thermally stressed steelhead were clustered and inactive in the shadows cast by large exposed boulders. They also lay at the heads of riffles under whitewater.

I considered bagging the trip and perhaps doing some high stream trout fishing while recrossing the Cascade Mountains to my home. But having traveled so far, I decided to think the matter through while dallying over a long lunch. Logic overcame dismay and I decided to play a hunch - that some fishing might be had from twilight on, if the water would cool sufficiently to de-stress the steelhead and stimulate them to move about in the pools.

I spent the rest of the day sketching the local landscape, and twilight found me in a long, boulder strewn pool that I had become familiar with on a previous trip.

A few minutes passed while I scanned the water. One fish broached, soon followed by another—my hunch had been a good one. I tied on a Royal Blue with a silver underwing, and began fishing.

Ten minutes passed and . . . "bam", a steelhead had solidly connected. Later, another fish followed suit—and so on that evening and the two that followed. The final tally: Nine fish hooked (all on the Royal Blue), five fish landed and released including a buck steelhead of sixteen pounds.

The trip home was filled with the joys of satisfaction.

## DARK PRIEST

A very early pattern of the series, Dark Priest seems more a reliable friend than an inanimate aggregation of hook, fur, and feathers. A longtime, consistent fly, it has earned more than it's share of battle stars. Though it has produced under a variety of conditions, this pattern does it's best work under conditions of subdued light and low light.

Another fish story is tempting here, but I'll let it pass in consideration of the reader's patience. Freely paraphrasing a maxim I but dimly remember: A thing overdone consumes one and one half times it's weight in others patience.

# The Low Water Series in Other Regions?

While this is a natural point to speculate on how my low water series might be applied to the salmonids of other places, I'll resist doing so. After all, these fish are distinct genotypically from summer steelhead of the Northwest. The rivers of other geographic areas differ in many ways from our western waters—run timing is different, and the seasonal conditions vary to some degree, at least.

Also, my experience with Great Lakes steelhead is nil. And in the case of atlantic salmon, my experience has been limited to the introduced fisheries of this species in certain lakes of Eastern Washington and Oregon.

Nonetheless, I cannot help but believe that the flat-winged low water steelhead flies would work well fished to these species.

My reluctance to extrapolate further is perhaps a good decision in another sense, for it will enable salmon and steelhead anglers in other places to experience the satisfaction of experimenting with the flies of this series without preconception. They can work out their own rationale for pattern selection under the various conditions they may encounter.

All twelve flies of the series have weathered the test of productivity. Over the seasons, certain of these flies have settled in my mind as "favorites"—trustworthy friends, as it were.

My hope is that you will test at least a majority of these patterns on the rivers you fish and form friendships with those which become your favorites. Wherever you fish them, may your casts be true and your hunches unerring.

*Perfection! Summer steelhead fresh from the sea  (R. Wahl c. 1950)*

*The inquisitive angler's bookshelf* (DBH photo)

*Wes Drain – a regular on the North Fork of the Stillaguamish River from the golden days of the early 1940's onward. (R. Wahl photo, 1967)*

# Dry Fly or Low Water Fly?

My strong preference for fishing with dry line techniques has been mentioned earlier in this writing. As the end of June approaches and the run-off swollen waters of the Northwest are dropping to summer levels, I develop a wonderful feeling of anticipation—for the best time of my fishing year is at hand. It is a time of summer steelhead charging my surface offerings and taking them in great swirls, with subtle slurps, or with graceful, classic head and tail rises.

Sometime in early July the water temperatures nudge into the 50's and I'm fishing low water flies and dry flies exclusively from then until the waters again become roilly and cold in late October.

On the river, I switch from dry fly to low water fly and back again as light conditions, water types, "hunches", and moods dictate. The past few years have found me fishing the low water fly slightly, but only slightly, more often than the dry fly. Experience has shown me that the low water fly is somewhat more effective over the whole range of summer and autumn conditions and water types.

There is little doubt in my mind that low water flies hold an edge over the dry fly when fishing to hatchery origin steelhead. Hatchery fish are generally more tentative in responding to on-the-surface flies than their wild counterparts.

Dry fly or low water fly? There is no conflict in my mind. The visual techniques, the well honed skills, the sense of competence involved in properly presenting both types of fly satisfy me greatly and bring me joy when I'm on the water.

## SPECIAL APPLICATIONS OF THE LOW WATER FLY

(1) When a steelhead rises to a dry fly and does not venture to take it. This often occurs as a series of surface swirls behind the fly as it crosses the stream. An immediate switch to a low water fly will frequently produce a solid take.

(2) When the sun is at or near the zenith under bright light conditions, the low water fly is usually more effective than the dry fly in my experience.

(3)  When water temperature drops down to the 50 degree mark or somewhat below, steelhead responding to a dry fly will often be seen turning well under the fly and returning to their lie. Substituting a well presented low water fly or wet fly fished off the dry line, two or three feet under the surface, will very often do the trick.

(4) Riffle-hitching a low water fly will oftentimes obtain a reaction from a dour or otherwise unresponsive fish. The heads of flies intended to be riffle-hitched should be tied longer than usual. This enables the hitch to be placed further back on the shank, thus causing the fly to more strongly resist the current with consequent greater disturbance to the surface—which is what riffle-hitching is all about. The hitch should always come off the shank in the direction of the angler. Having to retie the hitch every time one crosses to the opposite bank constitutes an annoyance that is a minor surcharge to fishing these feathered hydroplanes.

*Dick Van Demark demonstrates the Reverse or Galway cast which is delivered on the backcast – with the angler facing river bank (so the line can be seen and directed away from foliage) D.B. Homel photo.*

# Advanced Casting
## and the steelhead dry line method

Many years of experience cause me to believe that effective presentation rather than "killer fly patterns" is foremost of the factors that dictate fly fishing success.  It is convenient to think of presentation as consisting of two interconnected elements:

**(1)**  In-the-air-manipulations (employing various casting techniques).
**(2)**  On-the-water-manipulations (line and fly control).

Mastery of the dry line method requires competency in both.

In fishing both the low water fly and the dry fly, it is important that an angler be able to employ a variety of casts including **serpentine casts** (commonly called **S-casts**), **reach casts, reverse casts, curve casts, change of direction casts,** and **the double haul**.  He or she should also be capable of using these casts in an appropriate fashion as dictated by water speed, current patterns, angle of presentation, and location of bank-side foliage. I'm talking about advanced skills here, not rudimentary fly casting.

The <u>reach cast</u> can be executed both to the right and across the angler's body to the left (right-handed caster). It is, to my mind the most indispensable cast in dry line fishing because it greatly extends the drift of the fly and minimizes line mends. On a typical day of low water fishing, I use it to make eighty percent or more of my deliveries.

The <u>S-cast</u> is also very useful at times; for example when delivering the fly across a band of comparatively slow water into a band of fast water or vice-versa. S-casts can be accomplished in at least three ways, to my knowledge, but the easiest method is simply to "waggle" the tip of the rod when you have completed a high-stop delivery.

The <u>reverse</u> or <u>Galway cast</u> is useful when brush or trees are close behind you. It is also extremely useful when a brisk wind blows in the direction of the casting side of your body. Succinctly described, the reverse cast is executed by turning toward the shore and delivering the fly on the back cast.

The <u>change-of-direction cast</u> is also important when dealing with bankside foliage, and should be a part of your repertoire. This cast is executed by false casting parallel to the shore and changing the orientation of the wrist on the

*A properly executed reach cast at the moment of completion*

*Across-body reach cast performed by the author*

*The serpentine or S-cast (a very good slack line presentation)*

*The high stop. Elevated line and 10:30 position of the rod are demonstrated. (D.B. Homel photos)*

delivery, causing the line to angle across the stream.

Where significant distance is not a factor, the common <u>roll cast</u> is very useful when the angler is backed against a "verdant" shore.

<u>Curve casts</u> will come in handy (when presenting your fly underneath over-hanging foliage, for instance). It's a useful presentation to know, but not of overwhelming importance. The idea here is to "cant" your rod somewhat to the side, and then over-power your cast on the forward delivery, pulling back just as the line straightens out over the water. This causes the tip of the line to snap around into a positive curve cast.

The <u>double haul</u> takes considerable practice to master. It is best learned one step at a time. It tightens your loop, greatly increases line speed, reduces false casting, and makes long casting possible. The double haul will not only give you quicker delivery and more distant casts, when needed, but will also cut down on wear and fatigue of your casting arm. A single haul cast may suffice for intermediate distances and is better than no haul at all.

Well written, clearly illustrated instructions for the casts I have mentioned can be found in several books — the best of which include <u>Fly Casting with Lefty Kreh</u> by Bernard Kreh, and Joe Brooks' <u>Trout Fishing</u> (revised edition 1985).

Mastery of the *high stop* of the forward cast is an unavoidable precursor to proper execution of most of these various casts. By *high stop* , I mean checking or stopping the rod's forward motion at, or very near, the "ten-thirty o'clock" position. This causes the fly line to unfurl several feet above the water, and gives the angler time to perform various in-the-air presentations of the fly line.

Without mastery of the high stop, the angler is essentially limited to the straight line cast followed by standard line mends. With such a limited repertoire, effective fishing of complex currents and difficult lies is out of the question.

I would candidly urge serious anglers, who have not yet learned advanced casting skills, to consider engaging the services of a competent teacher of fly casting—either an experienced friend, a knowledgeable guide, or fly shop instructor having these abilities. Instruction should be one-on-one or one-on-two at most.

## THE DRY LINE METHOD

Lengthy discussion of dry line presentation and techniques is beyond the intent of this book, and has been competently treated in other writings such as Bill McMillan's book, <u>Dry Line Steelhead</u>. Bill's book provides comprehensive treatment of these subjects and, of the angling volumes and articles that I have read, ranks among the best of it's genre along with Trey Combs' two books, <u>Steelhead Fly Fishing and Flies</u> (1976) and <u>Steelhead Fly Fishing</u> (1991). I also wholeheartedly recommend the writings of Bill Bakke which have appeared in <u>Salmon, Trout, Steelheader</u>, and <u>Fly Fishing</u>, (formerly "Fly Fishing the West") magazines.

Your reading is not complete without thorough study of the classic book <u>Greased Line Fishing for Salmon</u>, compiled by "Jock Scott" from the fishing notes of A.H.E. Wood.

I will, nevertheless, throw in some summations that bear upon the subject:

(1) In general, the object of all presentations should be: [A], to cause the low water fly to travel at the same speed as the current during it's downstream drift, ideally more or less broadside of the current; and [B], to cause the fly to travel downstream as well as across during the swing.

(2) The preceding objectives can be accomplished by several methods. The method I most frequently use is to employ an in-the-air *reach cast* presentation followed by moving the rod downward and laterally so as to keep the rod tip in a position that slightly leads the line. When the rod is fully lowered and extended, I use short mends to feed line into the drift if needed.

(3) For those who struggle with in-the-air presentations, another method will suffice. In delivering the cast, purposely overshoot the intended drift of the fly by a few feet. After the fly
has settled on the water, raise the rod and pull
the fly back to it's intended drift. Use the slack
thus created to throw a hearty upstream mend,
or simply pick up the slack by raising the rod,
moving it upstream, and sitting the line down
again. Manipulate the drift of the fly as
described in paragraph two above. Obviously,
a similar technique can be used to accomplish a
**downstream** mend where required.

(4) In certain situations (for example, "streamy
water"), it is best to put the fly under tension
immediately after completing the cast, causing
it to wake in the surface film. The fly is best
worked with what I call *controlled drag* as it
swings across the current. Creating controlled
drag involves following the line with downstream rod movement and if necessary, feeding
line into the drift with quick, short mends to
slow down the fly's swing. Very often a riffle-
hitch is employed with this technique.

(5) The best fly patterns will be rendered largely ineffective by an angler's inability to read water, poor presentation, and poor understanding of the instincts and behavior of the quarry.

(6) A willingness to innovate and ignore some of what is known as conventional wisdom is essential to one's growth as a fly fisher. By doing this, one will attain full enjoyment of the many aspects of angling and will also keep the sport fresh and alive in his or her mind.

*This lively steelhead was most difficult to photograph in the shallows. (D. Van Demark)*

*Summer runs resting in a holding lie.  (R. Wahl photo)*

# *Reading Steelhead Water*

## *and some tactics to fish it*

## INTRODUCTION TO SEEING AND STALKING

There is no magic involved in learning how to read steelhead water. The real "secret" here is to possess an inquiring mind, eagerness to learn, and the patience to step-back from fishing and keenly observe what's happening around you—especially in the river. Anyone willing to persist is capable of mastering the tactics I will discuss in this chapter.

> *Eyes, ears and other senses + intuition and inventiveness + knowledge of habitat and quarry = fishing mastery.*

Once in the river, the steelhead only rarely is interested in feeding, if at all. Some writers disagree on the issue of whether or not steelhead actively feed while in fresh water. However, the consensus seems to be that steelhead "feed" for reasons of territorial defense or because of vestigial curiosity carried-over from smolthood. While I've not infrequently seen larval, pupal, and adult insects in a steelhead's stomach, it is also true that I have seen such unlikely "foods" as partially smoked cigars, wildfowl feathers, gravel, sticks, cigarette filters, and even a banana peel! An acquaintance claims to have found a grown water ouzel inside one particularly "glutinous" steelhead.

If we agree on this matter of a steelhead's indifference to food, then it is obvious that **the steelhead has no need to take up feeding stations.** Except when actively moving, the steelhead is going to be resting in *holding lies* —that is places where he is protected from predators, excessive light etc., and where he can rest with minimum energy expenditure.

### STEELHEAD MAGNETS

A venerable Northwest maxim has it that rocks are to steelhead as magnets are to iron filings. Steelhead anglers would be well advised to glue this pithy saying to the back of their eyelids! Brush piles, fallen trees, depressions in the stream bottom, log jams, and *seams* (which will be discussed later) are other steelhead magnets.

## SPOTTING STEELHEAD

It is nearly always a plus situation if you can spot your steelhead by stealthily walking the bank, and having located a fish, retreating to a fine and far-off position to make your presentation.

Simply spotting a steelhead in the water and casting to it, point blank, is rarely successful. On many occasions I go so far as to make presentations by standing in the upstream riffle or, on smaller rivers, even in the tail-out of the pool above.

## WADING

When wading, particularly while stalking a steelhead, beware of rocks that will roll under your weight. The rumbling crunch created by this effect can practically insure that every steelhead in the pool will be alerted to your presence. Whenever possible, wading for the purpose of positioning oneself to cast to a fish should be done in a soft, sliding, gliding movement.

## SEAMS

One of the more elemental but indispensable water reading skills is knowing how to recognize *seams*. Seams are caused by horizontal shearing of adjacent columns of water which are traveling at different velocities and exist as a discontinuity in the water flow. They are usually quite discernible once one knows what to look for. Succinctly stated, a seam

appears as an on the surface, irregular, wavering line oriented downstream and parallel to the direction of the flow.
Steelhead distributed throughout a pool will very often be
found just to one side or the other of a seam. Fish according-
ly.

Often, several seams will occur on a given piece of water at
various distances from the shoreline. The number of seams
are related to the differential velocity between the fastest and
slowest regions of current flow.

## SCOURED BOTTOMS

Where very strong riffles enter a pool, the bottom cobble
and rocks may be scoured for a considerable distance downstream. This presents an undesirable holding lie, as far as
steelhead are concerned, because the high degree of reflection from the soured surface offers no cover.

Steelhead will, however, often be found just below the
scoured area where *periphyton* (algae) cover the rocks and
provide low reflectivity and camouflage for the fish.

# WATER TYPES AND HOLDING LIES

## RIFFLES WITH DROP-OFFS

Drop-offs at the base of diagonal riffles are often superb

holding spots for steelhead. The fish may be found in surprisingly shallow spots whenever the surface flow of the riffle provides adequate cover for them. From the "drop-off" to several yards downstream exists a pocket of gently moving water, under the rapid surface flow, which creates a resting place for steelhead.

Riffles of this type are effectively fished by standing well up in the riffle and presenting the fly with ample slack line. Stop casts, S-casts, and reach casts all come into play here.

One unusual pool with these characteristics at it's head treated me to great fishing for many years. Curiously it has produced only at the drop-off and a few yards beyond, even though the pool is seventy five yards in length and appears to have other good holding water.

## RIFFLES WITH SLICKS AND POCKETS

Riffle sections having fair depth; and slicks and pockets created by chunky boulders or other obstructions, also hold low water steelhead well. Shorter casts and high-tipping the rod to lift the line over intervening currents, are often the order-of-the-day. The drift of the fly is often short and the casts many, especially in a short slick or pocket surrounded by extremely fast water.

The rise of the steelhead in foamy or streaking water of this type is sometimes exhilarating and at other times a complete surprise (where the bouncing water blurs your view). Landing the fish is frequently a matter of good fortune, as there are so many boulders for it to lodge the line or leader on. The experience is somewhat like participating in a "run-and-shoot" football offense.

## BROKEN WATER

Choppy water and streamy water are akin and may almost imperceptibly merge with the riffle and also into each other. In some pools, these water types constitute the greatest surface area. They also may represent the "honey" water or the pot of gold, if you will, in a steelhead pool.

The usual sequence in a pool is; riffle, choppy water, streamy water, mildly turbulent water, slower moving flats, tailouts or runouts, and on to the next riffle.

My impression is that choppy or streamy waters are fished well with waking type or skating type dry flies and with low water flies hitched or unhitched, during summer and early to mid-autumn.

## MILDLY TURBULENT AND FLAT WATERS

These waters will hold steelhead if sufficient cover (such as rocks and overhanging tree limbs) and current flow exists.

Fish holding in the flat of a pool from mid-season on can be outright dour or they may be skittish and reluctant to expose themselves—especially in bright light. It is often best to approach such water under the low light conditions of evening or morning, on cloudy days, when the water is in shadow, or during a summer rainstorm.

Mildly turbulent waters are not quite so difficult to approach. Both types of water require fine, far-off, and delicate presentations during the dog-days of summer. The fish will be spooky at best. Neutral or drab flies can be far more successful than high contrast or bright flies on these waters.

Dry flies dead-drifted, then swung across the even current, may be the answer at one time. Dry flies fished in a slow swing may be effective at another time. And at still another time, greased line techniques will do the job. On yet other occasions, nothing will be of any avail. Such are the vicissitudes of low water fishing.

## TAILOUTS

Under conditions of low water I have found tailouts especially productive during early morning and late evening, when steelhead are most apt to be moving upstream from one pool to another.

From my experience, the ideal tailouts have a cupped or concave bottom profile—which provides an immediate holding spot for fish tired from negotiating the riffle below. If the bottom of the tailout is not of this contour, then there is no calm place for the steelhead to hold underneath the fast water, unless sizable rocks break the flow.

Another configuration I've found favorable is one located above a funneled tailout (when the stream gradually narrows and speeds-up prior to entering the next riffle). This type of tailout often has a band of slower water to one side or the other of the funnel, providing a place for the fish to rest and recover.

## CORNER POOLS

Corner pools occur when the flow trends against the far bank and forms a sharp bend in the current, concentrating the moving water on the far side of the river. Such pools can create very difficult presentation problems because they usually have back eddies and/or an expanse of nearly slack water over which the cast must be made. Long mends, S-casts, or even up-stream presentations are the options if the eddy or slack water area is very broad.

## SLOW, DEEP POOLS

At times, especially during hot weather, whole schools of steelhead will often take up resting spots in deeper, flat water with slow currents. These fish can be difficult to entice. Over the years I have sometimes found it effective to fish a high riding steelhead dry fly dead-drift, occasionally punctuated by **subtle** skittering and popping of the fly so as to lightly disturb the surface. This should not be done to the point of spooking the quarry, but only enough to get their attention.

Another method of catching steelhead in deep, slow moving pools falls into the wet fly rather than the low water fly province—but is worth mentioning. This involves the use of a rabbit fur leech, weighted in the head and fished off the

*The "Maestro", Ralph Wahl conducting a steelhead symphony in 1955.*

floating line. The weighted leech is cast over and beyond a "pod" of steelhead, and brought back with a retrieve combining regular stripping motions accompanied by up-and-down flexing of the rod tip. This retrieve has an ability quotient equivalent to rubbing your stomach and patting your head. The results, however, are often resounding!

## JAMS, TREES, AND BRUSH PILES

Fallen trees, logs, and log jams frequently provide holding cover for one or several steelhead. In some cases these fish can be fished-to more or less conventionally; and in other cases they can't (that is, if the fish are underneath the jam or brush pile). Often, however, these unreachable fish can be had at dusk when they move out from under the cover and restlessly swim about the pool—as is their evening habit under low water conditions.

# SPECIAL CONDITIONS

## VERY LOW WATER CONDITIONS

Under very low drought conditions I find my efforts rewarded by concentrating on slicks and pockets in white water areas, at the base of such white water areas, or by fishing regular pools at night (legal in my home state). The white water breaks are best fished with a Wulff type steelhead dry fly or short, quick drifts with a low water fly.

## AUTUMN

When the fields have mellowed and water temperatures, as well as the bright leaves of autumn, begin to fall—I have often observed steelhead turning away from my surface presentations two to four feet under the surface. This behavior is probably related to a water coldness barrier. Research by Bill McMillan places this barrier at 44 degrees Fahrenheit (and I have great respect for what Bill says). My own personal experience would indicate 48 to 50 degrees as the practical downside borderline for effective on-surface and in-surface fishing. It has also been my observation that summer run steelhead tend to drop back further into the pools as the water cools to the sub-fifties and below.

When the water temperature dips into the forties and the fish's response becomes tentative or lethargic, I have found it practical to go to a heavier hooked wet fly. The wet fly is fished off the dry line and drifted a few inches to a couple of feet under the surface. Instead of "turn-offs", you will often get "turn-ons" with this technique.

## NIGHT FISHING FOR STEELHEAD

This experience can be downright surrealistic. A frantic steelhead leaping in the darkness. You try to guess it's location by the direction of the splashes. You are not able to keep a tight line—and you have no real idea where the line has been strung by the fleeing fish. Your knuckles have been bruised by the reel handle, your casting arm is about to fall off, and the steelhead is showing no signs of tiring or relenting. You scan the dim perspective downstream, hoping to divine the fishes location, and just at that moment the fish jumps directly up-stream of you! Minutes later you get lucky and fall on the fish in the shallows—your body so weak that it requires a real extraordinary effort just to remove the hook and release the fish unharmed.

Fantasy? No! The quasi-fictional account above distills the essence of many experiences with night hooked steelhead.

How is it accomplished? Take plenty of vitamin A to improve your night vision (or alternatively buy night vision glasses), have a mildly obsessive-compulsive personality, cast blindly, and use a dark (high contrast) low water fly for maximum silhouette. Also be prepared to sleep on the couch when you arrive home in the wee morning hours. And finally, don't say I haven't warned you!

## POST SCRIPT

Returning to this chapter's introduction, I expounded the belief that steelhead normally do not actively engage in fresh water feeding. There are exceptions, however, as the following anecdote will show.

Certain unusual strains of steelhead do feed actively while in the river and I've actually seen them doing it. These fish were certainly atypical, albeit very active surface feeders. A fish and wildlife biologist, to whom I inquired about this anomaly, explained it as a genetic adaptation of these particular fish in response to the several hundred miles they had to traverse to reach the spawning grounds.

It must also be admitted that I caught one of these fish using the ancient English technique of "dapping"—the first time, and very probably, the last that I will have cause to lure a steelhead with this celebrated technique.

*A worthy adversary released to fight again. (D. Van Demark photo)*

*"Putting Him Back"* (R. Wahl photo)

# *About Releasing Fish*

I am dismayed by the great number of anglers who have no idea how to properly work with exhausted, played-out fish—before releasing them. It is also distressing and not uncommon to hear anglers ardently and fervently engaged in well meaning discussions of the merits of catch-and-release with no real concept of when catch-and-release is appropriate and when it is not.

Regarding the first point made above, I wish to quote *How to Release a Fish* by Pete Caverhill. Pete is a fly fisher as well as a professional fisheries biologist of many decades experience with the British Columbia Fish and Wildlife Branch.

**(A)** *Play and release fish as rapidly as possible. A fish played for too long may not recover.*

**(B)** *Keep the fish in the water as much as possible. A fish may injure itself out of water, and scale loss is more likely out of water.*

**(C)** *Handle the fish gently with your bare, wet hands. Keep your fingers out of the gills, and don't squeeze the fish or cause scales to be lost or damaged.*

**(D)** *Remove the hook as rapidly as possible using longnose pliers. Be quick, but gentle. Barbless hooks are recommended. If the fish is deeply hooked, cut the leader and leave the hook in.*

**(E)** *Take the time to hold the fish in the water, moving it back and forth to pump water over it's gills. If fishing in a river, point the fish upstream while reviving it. When the fish begins to struggle and swim normally, let it go.*

Regarding the second point made in the introductory paragraph to this chapter, I believe the all or none approach to catch-and-release is not only foolish at both extremes—but also reflects ignorance of certain natural realities.

A much more realistic approach to catch-and-release, it seems to me, would be:

**(1)** Release all fish of wild origin. Surplus populations of wild steelhead stocks do not exist today.

**(2)** If one has the need to eat fish, take these fish from known hatchery stock (if legal), but do not take more than you have need for. Leave one for the next guy. However in rivers where both wild and hatchery stock are present, it is important to remove as many hatchery origin adults as possible by the end of the season to prevent cross breeding. This last statement obviously does not apply to streams where the recruitment of "wild" fish stems predominantly from hatchery parent stock (for example, the upper Columbia and it's tributaries).

(3) Blind release of all steelhead, regardless of origin, is contrary to fundamental biological realities. Hatchery and wild run steelhead are genetically dissimilar. Hatchery fish are maladapted to living in wild environments because of the genetic selection pressures which operate on them in the highly artificial conditions of hatcheries (i.e. the genetic effects of domestication).

The offspring of hatchery stock, when compared to wild stock, suffer a disproportionately higher mortality in a wild environment *during all stages of the life cycle*—from various causes.

A case can be made for the idea of limiting hatchery plants only to environmentally degraded streams having little or no spawning habitat remaining, and no longer harboring a viable wild population. A case can also be made for supplemental hatchery plants in rivers where overwhelming evidence shows that spawning and juvenile emergence timing does not encumber wild production.

**Bad things can happen when hatchery fish directly commingle with wild stocks:**

> Contamination and weakening of wild stock gene pools when hatchery X wild crosses occur.

> A seventeen year long study was conducted on Gobar Creek, a tributary of the Kalama River in Washington State. It demonstrated that allowing hatchery origin summer run spawners unrestricted opportunity to breed with wild stock, had a markedly adverse effect upon native wild stock over a period of years (ultimately driving the entire population to the zero point).

> Inter-specific competition between wild and hatchery juveniles for food, and habitat.

Competition for spawning habitat can occur when the reproductive timing of different strains coincides on the same stream.

Temporarily increasing the numbers of fish through admixing of hatchery juveniles with wild juveniles can strain the carrying capacity of the stream—with consequent increases in competition resulting in mortality to wild as well as hatchery stocks.

Introduction of diseases, carried by planted juvenile hatchery fish into wild populations. Indiscriminate planting of stocks from outside geographic regions also introduces new diseases to endemic populations.

I hope readers will consider the foregoing information as food for thought. It's not a matter of having an ax to grind, but rather my deep concern about the possible short and long term negative effects when hatchery origin fish are used to supplement wild stock production without a safe and sound biological plan.

Let us leave an abundant wild stock legacy for the generations of fishers and river lovers to come!

*"Off and Running". Walt Johnson with his hands full. (Columbia River below mouth of the Entiat – R. Wahl photo)*

# *Enthusiasm Rekindled*

With the crowding on most of our rivers having increased exponentially in recent decades, I am finding myself spending less time in pursuit of steelhead. Paradoxically, I seem to be enjoying it more than ever despite the sometimes subway-like conditions on the stream. I have been forced to increasingly refine my approach to angling, and I now move more slowly—feeling and seeing more while apparently doing less.

I often see anglers hurry past me, driven and grim with competitive urge; and I am saddened that they are missing the incredible, happy solitude that accompanies just being in and of a river and it's vibrant fringes.

With a rapidly increasing number of rivers being regulated for *wild fish release* or outright catch and release, my cynicism is mellowing as my enthusiasm is rekindled—for it is upon such rivers that I now predominantly fish. And if one chooses the right places and times, there are still opportunities to ply the waters with some degree of serenity and to fish runs and pools that aren't occupied from before break-of-day 'til darkness.

Maybe it is all working out for the best as I approach my declining years and, ultimately, that journey to a realm where the backcasts don't tangle.

*The late Enos Bradner, "Silver Fox" of the Northwest, tying-up a streamside special.*

# *A Look Back*

## *The Gestation of a Fly Fisher*

Fifty years ago at the impressionable, tender age of seven, I went fishing with a man named Don on a spring evening filled with light and, for me, a new type of adventure.

My gear on that evening consisted of an eight and one-half foot telescoping steel rod, a borrowed reel with level silk line, a three foot chunk of silkworm gut leader, and two Gray Hackle Yellow wet flies. The humble equipment and my first awkward efforts at fly casting, aided by the patience of my tutor, brought about an experience that was to change my life irreversibly—for two silver and incredibly wondrous creatures responded to my offerings. In retrospect, I realize that <u>both</u> the mystical creatures which had suddenly materialized out of the depths to take my fly in awesome swirls and the all agog boy on the other end were hooked simultaneously, very deeply hooked!

Sitting here at the typewriter; that spring evening re-materializes with clarity totally undiminished by the passage of years. It is a vision that exists both in past tense and present in my mind. Only sober logic jolts me back to reality . . . "that spring evening was a half century in the historical past."

It all happened on Barret Lake located a few miles south of the Canadian border in the northwest coastal region of Washington State - known to locals as the Fourth Corner. By good fortune, the small ranch where I grew up was but a short stone throw from the lake's shore.

One thing led to another and, with the help of my mentor, I was soon tying my own flies. I created simple hackled flies and hairwings with a cumbersome seventy-five cent vise and a few materials purchased from that great emporium of yore—Herters of Waseca, Minnesota (which at the time was the largest hunting and fishing supply house in the world).

A couple of years passed and my fly fishing arsenal had been upgraded to a genuine Heddon split cane fly rod, an Ocean City single action fly reel, double tapered Gladding silk fly line, and a Weber fly box filled with a somewhat respectable assortment of flies. I was now thoroughly committed to a lifetime as a fly fisher.

Other teachers of the art came to my home lake, taking time to show me things and offer advise. There was Audie Baxtor, Irv Fawcett, "Ace" Bellenger, and Fred Hunt, the finest caster around. There was also a soft-spoken, dry humored man by the name of Ralph Wahl (now widely known from his books, Come Wade the River, and One

Man's Steelhead Shangri-La), who years later was to become a close and valued friend—a friendship that exists to this day.

With this plethora of expertise and adult examples to emulate, my development as a coastal fly fisher advanced to a fair degree of competency at an age when most youthful anglers have not extended their piscatorial horizons beyond an awareness of the richest worm-digging grounds. More importantly, these men exposed me to the ideals of sportsmanship and to the ethics and broader values of the sport.

The early summer of 1945 stands out in my memory, for it was then that my original benefactor greatly expanded my world as it existed at the time—taking his son and me on a week long trip to the interior lakes of British Columbia and their fabled sedge hatches. This was followed a couple of summers later by a trip to Upper Campbell Lake on Vancouver Island, where I was introduced to an English-sounding gentleman named Roderick who loaned me a beautiful British fly reel when my own reel had developed problems. I clearly remember being awestruck by the power of the man's presence and personality while, at the same time, being attracted to his warmth and quiet humor. It was only years later that I realized this man was the renowned angling writer, Roderick L. Haig-Brown.

World War Two raged and ended, and soon thereafter new products and materials began to appear in the fishing magazines and mail order tackle catalogs: A new leader material called nylon; rods of an alien material known as fiberglass; synthetic fly lines that were guaranteed to sink or float without dressing (unheard of!); fly fishing vests to take the place of wicker creels and jacket pockets as tackle carriers; chest-high waders; and to us living in the western hinterlands, an entirely new type of fly, the nymph.

Many scoffed and most of us resisted these changes for a time, but eventually we succumbed to the advantages of the new products and the fishing horizons they opened. The task of soaking gut leaders overnight, and the laborious, endless greasing of fly lines (though viewed nostalgically by some today) were time consuming ordeals most of us are happy to see consigned to the annals of the angling past.

It was during this early post World War Two period, on an overcast November afternoon, that I "accidentally" hooked my first steelhead. At the time I was fly fishing for fall sea-run cutthroat—the steelhead was an early run winter fish traveling through Barret Lake on its way to the spawning tributaries. While my hands clutched the rod in a veritable death-grip, the monster towed me and my boat nearly a half mile down the lake.

I haven't been quite the same since!

*A 1967 photo of Walt Johnson, who pioneered the use of light line and the midge rod for summer steelhead in the late 1940's. (R. Wahl)*

*Three Musketeers of the "Stilly" – Porthos, Athos & D'Artagnon? No! It's Dick Van Demark, Walt Johnson and Ralph Wahl.*

# *Evening on the Methow*

I wade the lovely Orchard Pool beneath
the rimrock upward jutting as if
it meant to touch the pale ether
of sky above.

And all is still and peaceful
in the muted eventide—
save throaty call of great horned owl
echoing softly down the canyon wall,
and the swishing sibilance of supple line
cutting the faint purple of evening's holy light
to reach a subtle edge of current
beside a crescent rock.

I stand transfixed and happy
in that surreal gentian glow,
my senses full-opened to all about me.
The dusky fly—a tethered artifice
of fur and fancy—draws delicate tracings
in the thin rind of filmy surface.
A transient breeze descends,
sending a fleeting shiver of tiny rills
scampering down the shadowed pool.

The line arcs more quickly now
in the sliding current below.
A brief glint in the blue-black flow
signals my arm to move deftly
in baton master's stroke—
drawing smooth steel of hook into
a steelhead's gristled maw.

The circle, partly scribed,
is now completed and fulfilled . . .
A personal rite of communion has
returned me to a state of grace.

Dick Van Demark
Bellingham, Washington

# *Appendix 1*

## Construction and Use of a Spinning Block

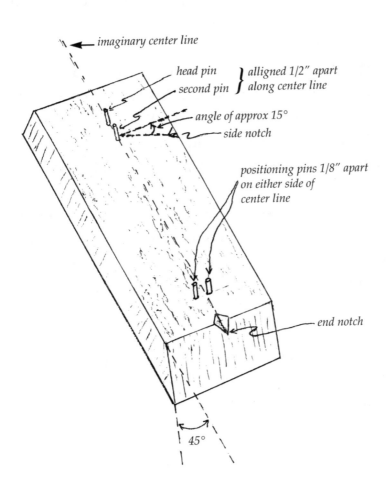

imaginary center line

head pin  } alligned 1/2" apart
second pin } along center line

angle of approx 15°

side notch

positioning pins 1/8" apart
on either side of
center line

end notch

45°

## NOTES

**(1)** The block is made from 1/2" thick wood stock (fir is a good choice). Cut the stock to a width of 2" and a length dependent on the length of the "flymph yarn" you wish to spin.

**(2)** The spinning block is quickly and easily made, not to mention inexpensive. I suggest you make several of various lengths. The 5" length (which makes a 4" long flymph yarn) and the 7 1/2" length (which yields approximately a 5 1/2" yarn length have proved most useful in my experience.

**(3)** Notches: Cut out shallow notches where shown in the diagram, then slice the bottom of the notched groove with a sharp razor blade. The notch eases positioning of the silk dubbing thread which is pulled down into the slice - that holds it.

**(4)** The pins are made from #17 or #18 brads which are pounded into the block in the positions shown in the diagram. The brad heads are then clipped off 3/8" above the block's surface.

## Use of Spinning Block to make spun Dubbing

Note: Use of waxed silk thread is strongly recommended. Other threads will often unravel when the completed spun fur body is removed from the spinning block.

**(1)** Cut a piece of silk thread which when doubled will reach from head pin on the spinning block to a point 1 1/2" beyond the end notch.

**(2)** Heavily wax the thread, then tie an overhand knot in the two loose ends to form a closed loop.

**(3)** Position the loop on the spinning block as shown.

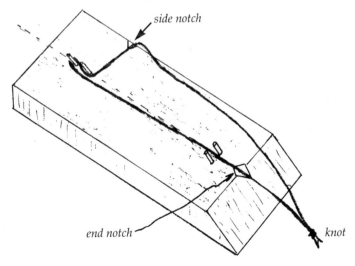

**(4)** Spread and arrange dubbing fur along the thread segment positioned along the center axis of the block.

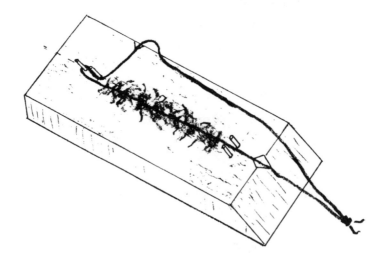

**(5)** Remove the thread previously placed in the side notch and place it on top of the dubbing fur. Pull the slack out of the thread.

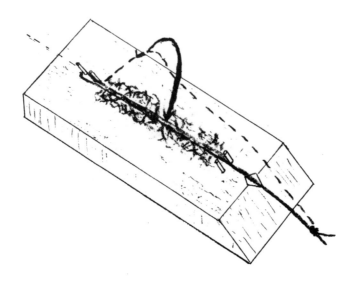

**(6)** Insert a "hook" made from a straightened paper clip (or a commercially produced "spinning tool") into the knot end of the spinning loop and lift the center thread out of the end notch. Keep a slight, but steady tension on the thread as this is done.

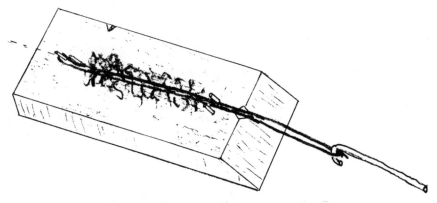

**(7)** Without releasing the tension, twirl the "hook" or spinning tool clockwise between your thumb and forefinger until you have a moderately tight twisted spun yarn with many fibers of various lengths sticking out.

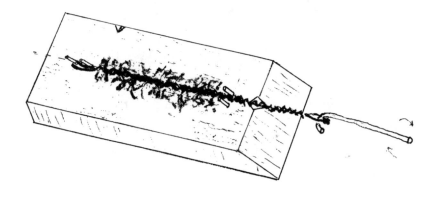

**(8)** Gently stroke out any loose fibers with your free thumb and forefinger without releasing tension on the silk spinning thread. Now remove the spinning "hook" from the thread loop. Then remove the entire piece of spun flymph yarn, you have created, from the spinning block. If you have used waxed silk as I've recommended, little unraveling will occur.

You may choose to make several spun fur bodies before commencing to tie flies. Simply store them on a piece of notched card as illustrated below. Bristol board makes excellent storage cards and is available at any store carrying art supplies.

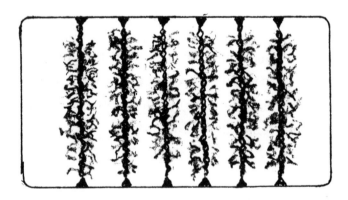

The classic book, <u>The Art of Tying the Wet Fly and Fishing the Flymph</u> (co-authored by Leisenring and Hidy), described the basic spinning block many years ago. It is my hope that the foregoing illustrations and notes help carry you through the steps necessary to efficiently creating better fly bodies using a block.

# *Appendix 2*

## Author's Equivalent Dubbing Formulas Using Synthetic and Organic Fur Mixes

BLOOD 'N BRANDY:  4 parts hot orange mohair, 2 parts scarlet (or red) mohair, 1 part florescent yellow-deep mohair.

BRAZEN LADY:  Not applicable as this pattern has a tinsel yarn body.

BRIGHT SIENNA:  2 1/2 parts fiery red-brown polyester, 1 part golden sienna polyester, 1 part hot orange mohair.

CREME-DE-MENTHE:  6 parts dark olive mohair, 1 part chartreuse rabbit.

DARK ALE:  Equal parts of dark brown mohair, dark brown polyester, and maroon mohair.

LOW WATER BEE:  Rear and forebody—equal parts of

brown mohair and dark brown polyester. Medial band—equal parts florescent yellow mohair and yellow polyester.

MAI TAI: 2 parts hot orange mohair, 1 part florescent yellow-deep mohair, 3 parts florescent red polyester, 2 parts maroon acrylic.

MOULIN ROUGE: 4 parts florescent orange mohair, 1 part scarlet polyester, 1 part florescent scarlet polyester.

OPTICAL BLACK: 1 part royal blue mohair, 1 part dark crimson mohair, 1 part viridian green polyester, 2 parts black polyester.

ROYAL BLUE: Rear half of body—royal blue mohair. Front half of body—6 parts scarlet polyester, 1 part yellow-medium mohair, 1 part florescent orange mohair, 1 part hot orange mohair.

TAWNY PORT: Step #1—blend 2 parts deep claret mohair and 2 parts maroon acrylic. Step#2—divide above mix into 3 parts. Add 2 equivalent parts hot orange mohair and 1 equivalent part florescent yellow-deep mohair. Blend.

DARK PRIEST: 2 parts black polyester, 2 parts medium dark brown polyester, 1 part maroon mohair.

**Improved (adjustable) Spinning Block ~** This improved block is a product of the inventive mind of Jack Salstrom of Bellingham, Washington. It enables the fly tyer to easily adjust dubbing loop length by moving the head pin forward or backward in a series of peg holes. The movable headpin allows one to create dubbing "noodles" in size increments between 4 and 8 inches in length. Jack is a handy person to know - he always seems to be able to come up with a better mousetrap.

# Wing and Hackle Materials

*From top to bottom in color plate 3*

**LEFT ROW** ~ (1) Grayish Chinese cock pheasant rump feather dyed red. (2) Brown Chinese cock pheasant rump feather. (3) Widgeon flank feather. (4) Long fibered, natural greenish-gray feather from Chinese cock pheasant rump. (5) Natural reddish-orange golden pheasant body feather. (6) Flank feather from a drake mallard or teal dyed hot orange.

**MIDDLE ROW** ~ (1) Golden pheasant tippet. (2) Golden pheasant tippet dyed scarlet. (3) Ruddy-brown shoulder feather from wing of golden pheasant. (4) Reddish-orange golden pheasant. (5) Pair of English grouse feathers.

**RIGHT ROW** ~ (1) Sample prepared "noodle" from the spinning block, for the *Creme de Menthe* . (2) Pair of greenish-gray feathers from the Chinese pheasant. (3) Pair of Mallard drake breast feathers dyed florescent scarlet. (4) Long fibered English grouse body feather. (5) Mallard flank feather dyed royal blue. (6) Chinese cock pheasant rump feather dyed black. Note also a sample of the copper tinsel yarn used for making the body of *Brazen Lady* .

# Blended Dubbing

*From top to bottom in color plate 4*

**LEFT ROW** ~ (1) Optical Black. (2) "Yellow" medial band for Low Water Bee; "brown" rear and forebody for Low Water Bee. (3) "Blue" rear half of body for Royal Blue; "red" front half of body for Royal Blue.

**MIDDLE ROW** ~ (1) Blood 'N Brandy. (2) Moulin Rouge. (3) Bright Sienna. (4) Creme De Menthe.

**RIGHT ROW** ~ (1) Mai Tai. (2) Dark Priest. (3) Tawny Port. (4) Dark Ale.

# Dick Van Demark

The author is a lifelong resident of the Pacific Northwest and a founder of the Fourth Corner Fly Fishers in Bellingham, Washington. He is a popular speaker at group meetings throughout the region, having developed slide presentations on the subjects of steelhead fly fishing, headwater trout angling, backroads Canadian fly fishing, and a conservation minded program about the sea-run cutthroat. As an accomplished artist and versatile angler, Dick divides his time between the studio, fly tying room, and numerous outdoor venues.

# Ralph Wahl

Mr. Wahl is considered to be the preeminent Twentieth Century fishing photographer in the black and white medium. All of Ralph's photographs were printed in his own darkroom under exacting conditions. His work has appeared in *Time, Life, Sports Illustrated, Field & Stream*, and *Fly Fisherman*.

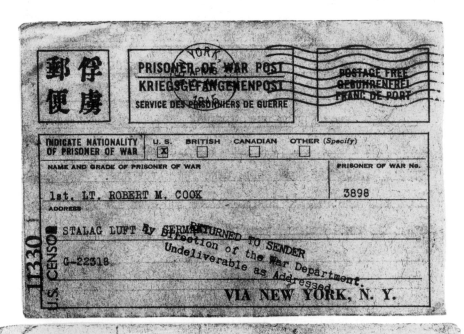

Bob Cook (Diane Van Demark's cousin) , a B-17 pilot, was shot down over Germany in 1944. His letter from Stalog Luft P.O.W. Camp indicates a strong desire to return home and get back to summer steelhead fishing on the North Fork of the Skykomish. Thoughts of casting to steelhead surely kept his spirits high those tough 15 months of incarceration. Note that he was forced to write a glowing review of conditions at the camp—otherwise his "hosts" would not send the letter!